FIGURED HARMONY AT THE KEYBOARD

R. O. Morris

PART II

OXFORD UNIVERSITY PRESS

INDEX OF SUBJECT-MATTER

PART I

PART II

PART II

THE EXERCISES in Part II, unlike those in Part I, will not for the most part be found capable of performance in close position throughout. The left hand will be called upon for more activity, and the student will need all his vigilance, for one does not at first 'feel' consecutives so readily when the forbidden intervals are divided between the two hands as when they all lie under the fingers of a single hand. Moreover, progressions that are correct in close position may become faulty when the change to open spacing is made.

Consider, for example, the following:

(1) shows a correct progression in close position. In (2) the spacing is open, and the progression is at once seen to be incorrect. In (3) the solution is given; if the first chord is taken in open spacing, the next one has to be taken close. Thus the performer must always be on his guard, ready to change from open to close positions, or *vice versa*, as circumstances require.

The chorales in § 1 and § 2 are all taken from the harmonized versions of J. S. Bach. For brevity's sake I have used numbers rather than names for the purpose of reference; the numbering followed is that of Breitkopf and Härtel's collection*, which is complete and easily accessible.

In one or two places I have slightly simplified a harmonic progression, not from any mistaken desire to improve on Bach, but because his manipulation of the parts is occasionally too intricate to be readily discernible by a beginner—or even a non-beginner—at the keyboard.

In performing these, the limits of the vocal compass must be borne in mind; the alto should never rise above *d*, or the tenor above *g*♯—and only seldom as high.

★ 371 Vierstimmige Choralgesänge von J. S. Bach

OXFORD UNIVERSITY PRESS, MUSIC DEPARTMENT, WALTON STREET, OXFORD OX2 6DP

§ 1. CHORALES WITH BOTH OUTER PARTS GIVEN

3

16

19

39
54
73

81

82

89

111

117

127
129
138

144

162

190

223

264

269

§ 2. CHORALES OF WHICH THE BASS ALONE IS GIVEN; THE TOP PART TO BE ADDED BY THE STUDENT AFTER HE HAS WORKED OUT A SATISFACTORY VERSION AT THE KEYBOARD

12

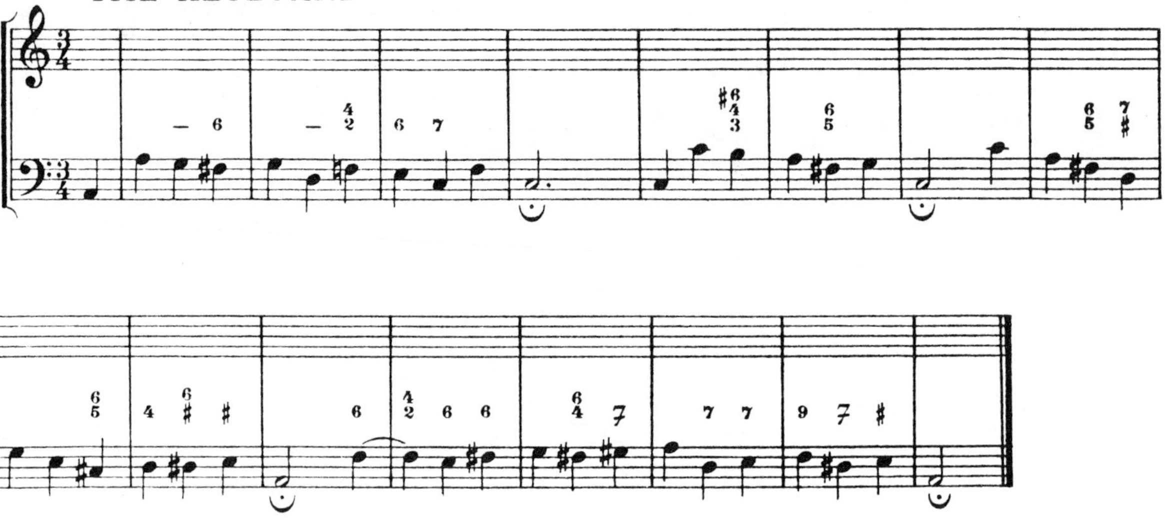

21

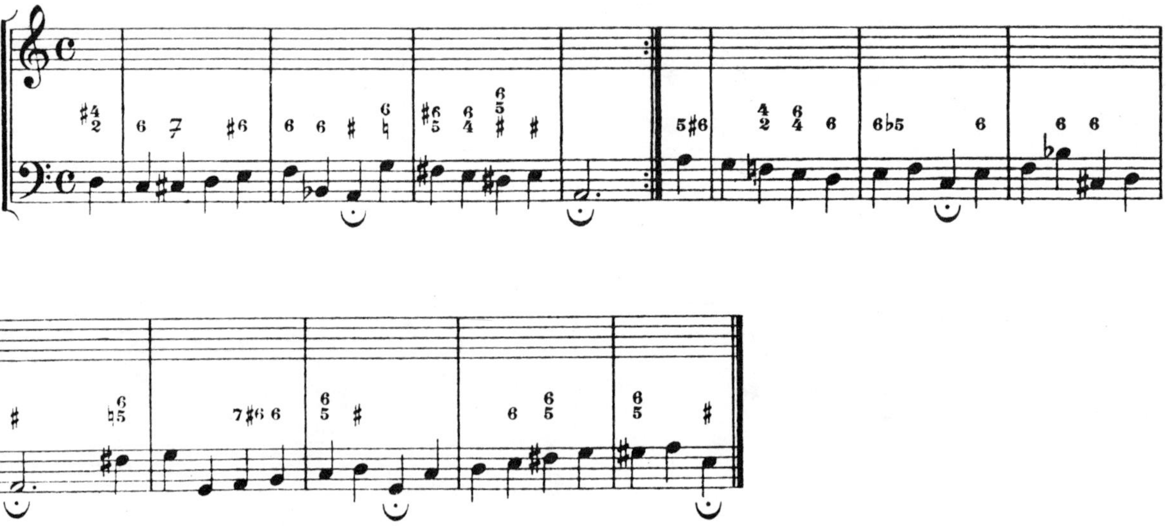

25

32
44
47
78

93
131
147

148
149
159
178

188

191

192

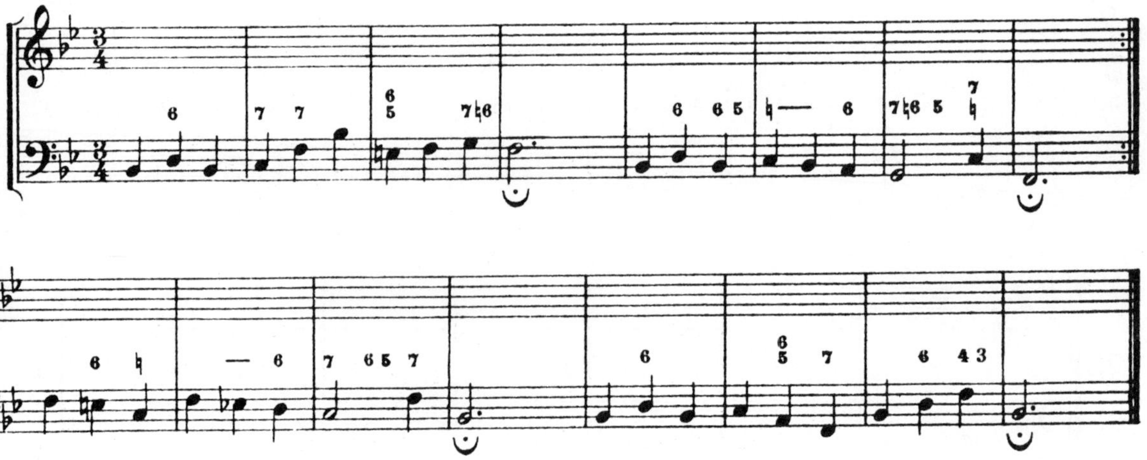

247
260
262

§ 3. MISCELLANEOUS BASSES

The following basses are somewhat longer and of a more varied character than those in the previous section. They are taken (with slight adaptations) from actual compositions, but are rather more fully figured than the originals. It must be remembered that the *continuo* player was not expected as a rule to play at sight from the bass alone. He had usually the score in front of him, or at any rate the principal melodic part or parts in addition to the bass. In this way many progressions were clear and obvious which might otherwise have been doubtful. Where (as here) the bass alone is given, the figuring necessarily has to be somewhat amplified.

Although reading from a bass alone quickens the mind and develops resourcefulness of finger, the practice of these exercises should by no means be confined to a single reading. On the contrary, each one should be studied and worked over again and again until the student is confident that he has found the most suitable positions and spacings of the various chords (i.e., those which sound best) and can give a really fluent interpretation of the figures before him. He should then copy out the top part which he has himself worked out, and play to his instructor from this copy.

It is not necessary that four parts should be maintained without intermission; it is often advisable to drop one part for a bar or two, for the sake of variety or to avoid congestion.

HANDEL

I

MENDELSSOHN

2

PURCELL

3

PURCELL

4

HANDEL

5

BACH

6

PURCELL

7

HAYDN

HAYDN

HANDEL

10

HANDEL

11

HANDEL

12

PURCELL

13

HAYDN

14

PURCELL

15

HANDEL

16

HANDEL

17

HAYDN

18

PURCELL

19

BACH

20

PURCELL

21

HAYDN

22

HANDEL

23

HANDEL

24

PURCELL

25

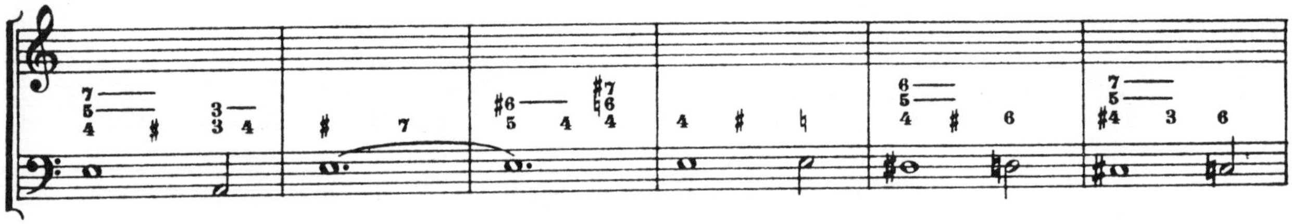

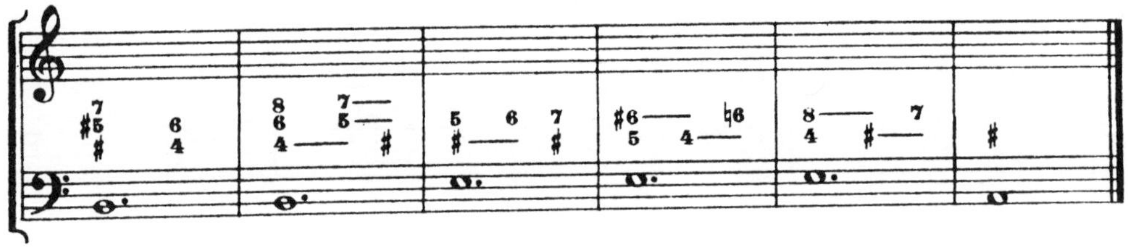

Reproduced and printed by
Halstan & Co. Ltd., Amersham, Bucks., England

OXFORD UNIVERSITY PRESS